The laws of the blades: the life philosophy of the blademasters

By Rick Bentsen
(As written by Solara Moonfire,
The High Priestess of the Blades)

Steel Drake Press
Taunton

The Laws of the Blades
The Life Philosophy of the Blademasters

For information, contact the author at
rickbentsen@rickbentsen.com

www.facebook.com/RickBentsenAuthor
www.rickbentsen.com

ISBN: 0998459828
ISBN-13: 978-0998459820

Praise for The Blademaster

"Up until I'd read "The Blademaster" by Rick Bentsen, the closest thing I'd come to reading or seeing a story in this genre was "The Lord Of The Rings" that I saw at the theater several years ago because my husband wanted to see it.

I wanted to read "The Blademaster" because Rick and I have been cyber friends since around 2000 and I wanted to support him and his new book.

So, kind of to my own surprise, when I started reading the saga of Alana Steeldrake (First Blademaster to be named in over 300 years) and Colwyn Starseeker (Protector to Alana Steeldrake and heir to the title of First Lord of the Valendale Territory) I found myself really enjoying it!

The story flows with just enough descriptions that keep the story moving and on course.

All the characters, even the secondary ones, are really well developed. I felt like I knew all the characters in the book, even the bad guys, by the time I'd finished it.

I'm impressed with Rick's writing ability. I'm amazed at his imagination. I'm intrigued with the names of places, characters, and phrases he came up with and how they perfectly fit the tone of the story. And I appreciated the underlying moral code of love and honor that he threaded throughout the story.

And I can totally see this story becoming a movie!"

--Pat Ballard, author (Abigail's Revenge, Wanted One Groom, and others... The Queen of Rubenesque Romances...)

Foreward

Greetings, Faithful Readers!

I am not sure how my readers will feel about this book. I worry that it will not be well received. I also worry that some of my readers might consider me a pretentious git trying to pass off a life philosophy on people. There are, after all, almost as many life philosophies as there are people. And it is fine if you think I'm a pretentious git. In a lot of ways, this book is for me more than anyone else. If that makes me overly pretentious, then so be it.

When I started writing The Blademaster Chronicles, I decided that my Blademasters should have a code to live by. A set of laws, as it were, that they would have to live by. And while, when I started, I did not set out to write all the laws out in a book form like this, I decided the time was right to do so.

I often talk about the various Laws of the Blades during author appearances. I have often said that the Law of the Blades is a set of laws that, should people live by them, would make their lives better. And that is true. The Law of the Blades makes up a life philosophy that could only improve someone's life were they to apply the philosophy to their lives.

In its simplest form, the Law of the Blades can be summed up by something we in geekdom refer to as "Wil Wheaton's Law".

Don't be a dick.

But really, it goes further than that. I often quote the First Law of the Blades to people. Or at least the basic gist of it. I tell people they should love each other and be kind to each other. And that is the basis of the entire Law of the Blades.

The First Law of the Blades reads: "You are commanded to love. Love your friends. Love your enemies. Love without reservation. Love without hesitation. Love without condition. Love without expectation of return. If you must fight, then fight with love in your heart. If you must kill, then kill with love in your heart. Never kill or fight with hate or anger in your heart. Hate leads to impotence, but love brings power. This is the law a Blademaster must live by more than any other or else she will be powerless to serve as she should. It is the First Law of the Blades because it is the most important. Live by it, or you will die."

I knew from the start that I wanted this message to be the basis of The Blademaster Chronicles. I knew that I wanted to show the power of love in a person's life. And what better way to do so than to have a main character whose abilities are fueled by love? Love, given unconditionally is, I think, the most powerful magic in the world.

Back in 2016, my daughter Kaitlyn interviewed me for a school project. She was tasked to interview someone that she admired and thought was interesting. The interview was designed to draw out the subject's story. Well, I agreed to participate even if I didn't think my story was all that interesting. It's the stories I tell in these books that is the truly interesting part of my life. But I love my daughter and so I said yes.

The first thing she asked me was "What is your life quote?" Now... I want you to think about that for a moment. If someone were to ask you "What is your life quote?" what would you answer them? Right. It's not something you actually think about. So I had to think about this for a while. And I came up with something. I wasn't sure about the quote at first. I felt like I had just talked out my butt as anyone who knows me can tell you that I am known to do. But the more I read the quote, the more I realized that it is, in fact, my life quote. And it is really a quote which explains the whole purpose behind the Law of the Blades.

I wrote this: "In the end, we are defined by our capacity to love, because I believe love to be the most powerful force in the world."

I truly believe those words. It is worth noting that many people feel this way. The world would be a whole lot better if everyone just loved each other a little more.

The Law of the Blades is meant to be a guide. A set of principles that would make a person's life better if they followed them, as it were. It is a life philosophy that I am trying to apply to my own life. And so I decided that I should put out a book laying out the Law of the Blades so that other people could benefit from this life philosophy.

The question then was how to go about writing it out? I mean, I could just write the various Laws and be done with it. But that would be a very short book. Besides, all the Laws that have been released in the books so far are already in the appendix at the back of each book in The Blademaster Chronicles. So how could I make this special?

And then I hit on a wonderful idea.

I could write the book from the point of view of Solara Moonfire, the High Priestess of the Blades. I would write it out in her words as if she were explaining all of the Laws of the Blades. I would write it as if she were writing it while waiting for the very first Blademaster to arrive at the Temple of the Blades.

Of course, that led me to a new problem. If Solara wrote this out in book form... why do none of the Blademasters have a copy? It's a good question. And I do have an answer. Solara decided that, while she would write the Law of the Blades down along with her thoughts about the various Laws, it would be up to each of the individual Blademasters to learn the Laws as they go. And how to apply those Laws to their own lives. It is possible that this will change in the future, but, for now at least, Blademasters need to learn on the job.

So, having decided how I was going to do this book, and then deciding how I was going to resolve the issue that I, inadvertently, created by deciding how I was going to do this book, I set to writing it.

I hope that you enjoy learning the full Law of the Blades and why Solara thought that each of these laws were important. And I hope that you will apply some of these things to your own lives.

As Wil Wheaton says in his law, "Don't be a dick." And as I say in mine, "Be kind to each other and give some love whenever possible."

I love you all,
Rick Bentsen
December 9, 2017

Acknowledgements

I can hear it now. "Oh, goodness me, the author is about to blather on and on about who did what to help him... Do we really have to read this?" First of all, I love the word blather and I now firmly promise to use the word far more often.

Second, no, you don't have to read this. But I would be remiss if I did not include my thanks. So, yes. Feel free to skip this section, but I shall now blather (told you I would use the word more often) on about Team Rick Bentsen and all they've done.

First of all, thanks to God for the gifts that make the writing possible. A little bit of imagination goes a long way, it would seem.

To my parents, who have been arranging many in person appearances for me to sign and sell my books. It has been a very interesting journey over the past several months, but I have enjoyed every bit of it.

To my brother without whom I would likely never have been introduced to Dungeons and Dragons. Without which.... No Blademaster.

To my continuity expert and editor, Joanna, for everything she does. As I said in *The Blademaster*, Joanna knows the characters as well, if not better, than I do. It makes it easier to hand these books off to her when I know she will take good care of them.

To my daughters, Hailey and Kaitlyn, for helping to open my heart back up. Were it not for them, this story likely never would have fully happened.

To Anna for helping me through a very very difficult time in my life and for brightening my life just by being the bright and beautiful person you are. The love you have given me when I needed it means more than you could ever know. Thank you. And I love you.

To my readers, because without you, there would be no point to doing this. I love each and every one of you.

Finally to Alana and Colwyn. You came into my life like a whirlwind and have made the past several years very interesting. You two are very special to me. Thank you for letting me tell your story to the world. For without you two, there would be no Law of the Blades to share.

.

*For the woman who helped me
to understand the true meaning
behind the Law of the Blades.
I love you.*

the laws of the blades

the life philosophy of the blademasters

Contents

ᴛo ᴛhe blademasᴛeʀs

am the Lady Solara Moonfire. Once I was a warrior dedicated to our Lord Taelin. Now, I serve Lord Taelin as the High Priestess of the Blades. It is my job to oversee the Temple of the Blades as well as ensure the Blademasters have all they need to fulfill their duties to the Southern Dales. It is a very important responsibility and one that I take in service to Lord Taelin.

I sit, now, in my sanctuary and wait for the first Blademaster to arrive. I know that the Blademaster has been found and is on her way. As I wait, I find myself contemplating the future. I know that the Blademasters are important to the protection of the Southern Dales. And yet, I fear that we do not yet know exactly what we are unleashing on the world.

The Blademasters need to have a code to follow as they go through their activities. As I sit here in my sanctuary, I feel like I need to create that code. And so, what follows shall be known as the Law of the Blades. I do not know, yet, exactly what this Law of the Blades will entail, but it is my hope that the Law of the Blades will ensure that the Blademasters have all they need in order to fulfill their duty to the Southern Dales.

Lord Taelin has deemed that the power of the Blademaster be based on the power of love. This, I hope, will ensure that the Blademasters will strive for the light, as love is a force of goodness. Indeed, it is, in many ways, the most powerful magic in the world.

Life and love are precious things. And the Blademasters are to be the protectors of both. It is my hope that the words I am about to write will aid the Blademasters in that task.

And so, with the flip of the page begins the Law of the Blades. Heed these words, Blademasters, for they will guide you in all you do.

The First Law of the Blades

ou are commanded to love. Love your friends. Love your enemies. Love without reservation. Love without hesitation. Love without condition. Love without expectation of return. If you must fight, then fight with love in your heart. If you must kill, then kill with love in your heart. Never kill or fight with hate or anger in your heart. Hate leads to impotence, but love brings power. This is the law a Blademaster must live by more than any other or else she will be powerless to serve as she should. It is the First Law of the Blades because it is the most important. Live by it, or you will die.

All truth and all philosophy must begin somewhere. In that, all are in agreement. And so must the Law of the

The Laws of the Blades

Blades begin with the most simple of Laws. It is simple, yes, but it is the most important. All of the remaining Laws of the Blades build from this one Law.

It is no mistake that Lord Taelin has based the power of a Blademaster upon the power of love, for love truly is the most powerful force in the world. Love is the force that shapes the world, and it is only through love that the world continues to exist as we know it. It is because of love that future generations are born into the world. And so, a Blademaster must live in all they do in a spirit of love.

It is for this reason that the Blademaster must marry her true love. Her true love, once married to her, shall be known as her Protector. The Test of the Blades, while it has the potential to be damaging to the psyche of a Blademaster should she lose multiple potential mates in the Test of the Blades, is imperative to ensure that the Blademaster finds their true love, for only in the bonds of true love can the Blademasters have the full protection offered by that force.

It gives me no joy to force potential Protectors to the Blademasters to undergo the Test of the Blades. But it is the only way to ensure the sanctity of the bond.

The term Protector is, perhaps, not the most accurate way to describe the Blademaster's mate. It is not the man that a Blademaster marries that is her protection. It is, instead the bond of love that she shares with her Protector that shall be her protection. That is why it is so important to find the right person.

In the love between a Blademaster and her Protector lies the most powerful force on Calthea. It is within this bond that a Blademaster must act. By doing so, she ensures that she acts as Lord Taelin would expect her to. By doing so, the Blademaster will act in the best interest of Calthea.

The enemy will act in hate. Love is the only counter to hate. Love is balance. Hate is without balance.

This is the First Law of the Blades because it is the most important. All of the other Laws of the Blades build off this one. Without acting in love, a Blademaster cannot hope to follow the remainder of the Law of the Blades.

the secon∂ law of the bla∂es

rue love breeds true forgiveness. Nothing is more powerful than the ability to forgive the one you love. And nothing brings you closer than the forgiveness of your own misdeeds.

As we go through the Laws of the Blades, it be important to note that the Laws tend to build off each other. The Second Law of the Blades directly builds off the First Law of the Blades. So to, as will become clear later on, do other Laws build upon the Second Law of the Blades.

There is a magic in forgiveness just as there is a magic in love. The two magics are bound together for you cannot have forgiveness without love. In the end, you cannot have love without forgiveness either.

The Laws of the Blades

It is especially important for a Blademaster to be able to forgive her Protector should he wrong her in some way. As previously discussed, the true protection for a Blademaster lies in the bond of love she shares with her Protector. It is, therefore, of the utmost import that she be able to forgive him for wronging her.

Forgiveness, in the end, will keep the Blademaster as safe as love will. Failing to forgive a wrong can lead to a festering grudge. Such a grudge can only hinder the bond of love. It is imperative to avoid such a grudge.

But even more than that, communicating about and forgiving such wrongs will bring two people closer.

It does not matter if it is the Blademaster's Protector or if it is anyone else in her life. She should strive to forgive their wrongs.

And she should hope for a reciprocation of such forgiveness should she wrong someone else, for a Blademaster will not be able to do what is right without wronging others.

It is possible to not make a mistake and still wrong someone by doing the right thing. A Blademaster cannot worry about wronging others in the execution of her duties. Instead, she should focus on doing the right thing, no matter how much it may hurt someone else. She should, then, seek forgiveness from those she may have wronged.

This is, perhaps, the hardest of the Laws to properly apply to one's life. It is a hard thing to do to forgive others for wronging you. It is harder still to seek forgiveness for things that you have done for others. I know it is hard. But I can only stress how important it is.

The Third Law of the Blades

ark and light. Good and evil. Black and white. These are two sides of the same coin. Both sides must exist or neither will.

The Blademasters are the chosen warriors of Lord Taelin, who is also known as the Lightbringer. As a result, the Blademasters serve the Light. They will often, in fact, be referred to as Children of the Light.

But as Lord Taelin is the Light, so too is Thraal known as the Dark God. You cannot have a light without a dark to stick it in. There is no good without evil to counter it.

This is a natural law as much as it is a Law of the Blades. It is not the Blademasters' job to eradicate the darkness, for they cannot do so. It is, instead, their job to be the light against the darkness; to be the goodness that counters the evil in the world.

Much will be spoken of in the Law of the Blades about balance. Balance is a greatly important concept for the Blademasters. The Blademasters are the balance to the forces of the Dark God. They must never forget that they are the counter to the darkness, nor must they ever forget that the darkness must exist for them to counter.

ℭhe ℱouℛℭh law
oℱ ℭhe blades

P ower is not given to those who seek it.

There are many different types of power. There is political power, magical power, the power of life and death. And there are still further types of power.

All of these types of power have in common that power tends to go to those who do not seek to have it.

There is a simple reason for this truism. Power in the hands of the wrong person will be misused. A person who seeks out the power of life and death is as like as not to be corrupted by that power and start to kill indiscriminately.

There is a truth that was written a long time ago that says power corrupts and absolute power corrupts absolutely. These words are true. The power of a

The Laws of the Blades

Blademaster, were it to be put in the hands of the wrong person, would absolutely corrupt them. For this reason, the women who are to be Blademasters shall be called rather than to be something that a woman should aspire to. Considering that they are making decisions for other people by becoming a Blademaster, it is important that only the right people are chosen.

the fifth law
of the blades

lways be prepared, for an attack may come at any moment.

A Blademaster must remain always vigilant. She must always be cognizant of her surroundings. As the chosen warriors of our Lord Taelin, the Blademasters will constantly be targets of attack for the forces of the Dark God.

Only by being constantly vigilant and always ready for such an attack can a Blademaster hope to stay alive.

This is, perhaps, the easiest Law to understand while at the same time the hardest Law to apply. It is difficult to stay constantly at the ready for an attack, it is true. But the Blademasters and their companions must adhere to this Law. Failure to be constantly cognizant of what is

The Laws of the Blades

going on around the Blademaster can result in her death or
the death of her companions.

The sixth law of the blades

I n all that you do, always remain true to yourself. Do not let others change your path or how you do things. Believe in yourself and do things as you feel you must.

In many ways, this is the second most important Law of the Blades. It is built off the First Law of the Blades, in that it involves a Blademaster loving herself.

The world will try to change a Blademaster from being the Child of the Light that she is. No matter what happens, a Blademaster must believe in herself and her abilities, and she must remain true to who she is.

If she allows the world to change her or force her to no longer act as she normally would, she will lose her way.

The Laws of the Blades

Love is, as has been mentioned before in the Law of the Blades, the central core of a Blademaster's power. Love of herself is very much a part of the magic. Love of herself should not, however, be the most important love she experiences, or she will be just as lost. But she must respect who she is and she must not let anyone change who she is, or she will be unable to fulfill her role in life.

the seventh law of the blades

Sometimes, despite all the skill that a Blademaster possesses, she must still depend on a little luck from time to time in order to make it through.

As much as the Blademasters are the creation of the Lord of Wisdom, they are also the creation of the Lady of Luck. As they were created out of the love between Lord Taelin and Lady Laeyra, it only stands to reason that the Blademasters must depend both on the wisdom of Taelin and the luck of Laeyra as they go through their lives.

In many ways, luck could be considered blind chance. And it is true that some luck is exactly that. But a Blademaster can manipulate the luck she experiences to a degree.

The Laws of the Blades

By arming herself with her experience and with wisdom, she can, possibly, cause a positive shift in her fortunes.

In its ultimate form, however, luck is a greatly random thing. It is best for a Blademaster to prepare the best she can and hope that, when luck is required, it will favor her.

the eighth law
of the blades

henever possible, do your best to provide aid and succor to those who need it.

The Blademasters serve the Southern Dales. A part of that service is to provide aid and comfort to the residents of the Southern Dales.

This is something that the Blademasters must be prepared to do at any time. The lives of the residents of the Southern Dales are to be protected whenever possible. To that end, the Blademasters must be prepared to render aid whenever possible.

Aid and comfort come from love and are some of the greatest gifts that the Blademasters can give to the people of the Southern Dales.

The Laws of the Blades

the ninth law
of the blades

Blademaster's word is her bond. Never break a vow. Always honor your agreements. Always follow through on your promises.

As with all things in a Blademaster's life, she should approach any vows that she makes with honor. It is important for a Blademaster to keep her word at all times.

A Blademaster should not make promises that she is unwilling to follow through on. Further, she should always speak the truth about an agreement. If she cannot follow through on something she has agreed on for some reason, she should be honest about the reason why and find a way to fulfill the agreement at a later date.

The Laws of the Blades

Honor and respect will help a Blademaster to keep her vows.

ᚦhe ᚦeᚾᚦh law
oᚠ ᚦhe blades

Blademaster has a voice of authority. Her voice must never be used for personal gain. As with all of her other abilities, it must only be used to serve the balance. Should she misuse her voice of authority, as with any of her other abilities, it will cause her to stray from her path.

All of the Blademaster's abilities have the potential to be misused if she is not careful. While this particular ability has no less potential for misuse, the voice of authority is an ability that should be especially guarded.

Because of the unique position that a Blademaster holds in the Southern Dales, it is only natural that others would listen to her voice when she speaks. Therefore, a

The Laws of the Blades

Blademaster must always be careful about how she uses the voice of authority that she has.

As will all of her other abilities, the Blademaster must use this one only in a way that directly helps her in her service to the Southern Dales.

A Blademaster must only use her voice of authority if it will help others.

The eleventh law of the blades

ife is precious. By serving the balance and the Southern Dales, the Blademasters are charged with the preservation of life.

All life is precious. Not just the lives of people that the Blademasters care about. The lives of the people that the Blademasters must fight are precious as well.

The Blademasters must fight with love in their hearts, remembering that life is precious. If a Blademaster must kill one of their opponents, it must be because there was no other option open to them. Killing is the last resort for a Blademaster, or at least it should be.

Respect for life comes from love. As I have discussed before, love is the basis of all of the Laws of the Blades. By

The Laws of the Blades

keeping the First Law of the Blades in her heart, a Blademaster should find it easy to respect all life.

Other Laws build off this one, just as this Law builds off the First Law of the Blades. By keeping one, a Blademaster should be able to keep all.

The Twelfth Law
of the Blades

estiny is what a person makes of it. Prophecy, if used correctly, can be an aid to a Blademaster, but it is her free will that must guide her. A Blademaster must use all aids at her disposal when making a decision, but she must be guided, in the end, by her own reason, wisdom, and free will.

It is important for a Blademaster to use everything at her disposal when faced with a decision that she has to make. But it is equally as important to ensure that she not focus on what may or may not be written as what has to happen. Free will is important in making decisions.

A Blademaster must depend on her own wisdom and free will in order to make the correct decision.

The Laws of the Blades

Free will is the counter and the fulfillment of destiny. This seems counterintuitive, but it is also true. A Blademaster cannot fulfill destiny without making a conscious decision to.

The future, although it may be predicted, is not set in stone. Future events are affected by the choices we all make.

The Thirteenth Law
of the Blades

A Blademaster should treat everyone with respect. She should respect the authority of those who do have authority over her. Whoever a Blademaster comes into contact with should be treated with the same respect and courtesy as the Blademaster herself would wish to be treated.

The Thirteenth Law of the Blades builds directly from the First and Eleventh Laws. If a Blademaster treats everyone she comes into contact with in a spirit of love and believes that all life is precious, then it will be easy for her to treat everyone with the respect they are due.

There should be no difference in how a Blademaster treats someone that is in a position of leadership over her, such as myself or the King of the Southern Dales, than how she treats someone she is trying to aid. All life is sacred and everyone should be treated with the same respect.

There will be people that a Blademaster comes into contact with that she will have a hard time treating with respect. The right thing to do is not always easy. But it is always the right thing to do to treat everyone with love and respect, not just the people that a Blademaster likes.

The Fourteenth Law of the Blades

here are many things in life that are but mere illusions. Things are not always as they appear. A Blademaster must depend on the wisdom of Taelin to understand what is real and what is an illusion. Confusion brought on by false realities can lead to a gruesome death. Always remember to let Lord Taelin be your guide in everything you do. Remembering this will cause you to see through any illusion that is in your path.

Lord Taelin is known as the Lord of Wisdom. Wisdom and knowledge must always be a Blademaster's guides through life. The Dark God will attempt to twist reality so as to confuse you.

Remain in the Light of Taelin and you will be able to see through any illusion the Dark God puts in your path.

But the Dark God is not the only danger that this Law applies to. Many things that the Blademasters will encounter will not always be as they seem upon first look. Wisdom and knowledge will be your guide through those things. A Blademaster must carefully examine all that they come in contact with so that they will know what is real and what is not as it appears to be.

When all else fails, seek out the guidance of your Lord Taelin as Lord Taelin's wisdom will always guide you to the correct reality of a situation.

The Fifteenth Law
of the Blades

I n life as in battle, there are no guarantees. Victory and defeat teeter on the edge of a thin blade. It is belief in one's self that can make the difference between victory and defeat. A Blademaster must always believe in herself and be willing to seek the help of others in order to claim victory. This is the truth of life and battle. Live or die as you choose.

A Blademaster must always believe in herself and her abilities. It is not always easy to do so, and there will be times where you will doubt your abilities. In those times, seek solace in the balance and in your Lord Taelin and Lady Laeyra. They will guide you in all that you do.

But, as much as a Blademaster must believe in herself, she must also know when to depend on others. There will be a great deal that the Blademasters will face that they will not be able to do on their own. There will be situations where they will have to send others to do things for them. There will be times where they will have to completely depend on others to accomplish things that they cannot on their own.

A Blademaster must realize when she can do something on her own and when she must depend on someone else in order to accomplish her goals.

She must, therefore, be able to ask for help when the time arises. A part of the reason that the Blademasters must marry their true love is so that they will always have one person that they can count on to help them whenever it is needed.

The sixteenth law of the blades

Blademaster's mind needs to be as sharp as her body's skills and her blades.

While it is important for a Blademaster to keep her skills and her blades sharp, her keenest weapon will always be her mind. Her mind is what will allow her to employ all of her other skills.

More, keeping her mind sharp will allow her to reason out solutions to problems that arise during the course of her journeys. There will be a great many problems that will come up for the Blademasters that their blades will not be able to solve. As such, it is imperative that their minds stay sharp.

Lord Taelin is one of the patron deities for the Blademasters. As he is the Lord of Wisdom, it is no surprise that the Blademasters should keep their minds sharp. Lord Taelin values wisdom and knowledge, and so should his chosen warriors.

To that end, the Blademasters should exercise their minds as much as they exercise their bodies and their skills. They should meditate to clear their minds whenever they have the opportunity to, and they should always take the opportunity to soak up new knowledge that comes along whenever possible.

the seventeenth law of the blades

A Blademaster should always seek to speak the truth of a situation. There is no guarantee that the message will be heard. A man who does not wish to believe the truth will not hear it. Likewise a man not willing to help himself cannot be helped by others.

As the chosen warriors of our Lord Taelin, the Blademasters should always seek to be a beacon of light in the world. In that, the Blademasters should always seek to always speak the truth of a situation. A Blademaster cannot serve the Southern Dales by speaking falsehoods.

In truth, if a Blademaster is acting in the way of the First Law of the Blades, they cannot speak in falsehoods, for lying is anathema to love. By its nature, love requires honesty.

The Laws of the Blades

Honesty can be a tricky thing, however. Just because a Blademaster speaks honestly about a situation does not mean that that truth will be accepted by the listener. All the Blademaster can do is keep speaking the truth. It is incumbent upon the Blademaster to always focus on the truth of a situation. She should do all she can to help the listener to understand the truth, but she should know that the listener may never accept the truth of the situation from just her words. It is the way of the world.

Likewise, a Blademaster should always endeavor to help others. This is, after all, the primary edict of a Blademaster. It is true that a person cannot truly be helped unless they are willing to help themselves, but a Blademaster must always be ready to lend aid to anyone in need. Whether or not that aid is accepted, it must be offered.

the eighteenth law
of the blades

In all of life, there must be balance. To lose that balance is to invite chaos and death in. A Blademaster must always be in balance in herself and in her dealings with others. That is why the First Law of the Blades is so important. The love she shares with her husband must balance the death she must deal in her position.

Much has already been said about balance and love in these pages. Before I end my thoughts on the Laws of the Blades, I am sure to touch on both again. Balance and love are the two cornerstones upon which the power of the Blademasters is built.

A Blademaster must remain in balance within herself. She must focus on the bond of love that she shares with her husband. It is her protection and the base of her power. Losing that bond of love in any way will cause her to become unbalanced and her abilities will falter.

Likewise, a Blademaster must be balanced in her dealings with others. She must always deal with others with love and gratitude, and she must seek forgiveness whenever she wrongs someone else, and she must be willing to forgive others when they wrong her. She must be willing to seek help from others and she must help others when she can.

It is this sense of balance, combined with the love she shares for her Protector, that will keep a Blademaster from falling off the path of the Light.

the nineteenth law of the blades

e all make mistakes. The true test of a person is their reaction to making a mistake. Only by accepting the mistake and doing one's best to make amends can a person keep on the correct path.

Allow me to be clear on this matter. Every Blademaster that serves the Southern Dales will, at some point, make a mistake. Probably more than one. It is simply the nature of mortal beings. No one is perfect, and the Blademasters are not exceptions to that rule.

Knowing that all Blademasters will make mistakes, it is important that they be able to recognize when they have made an error and respond accordingly. In a way, this Law ties into the Second Law, for a Blademaster should seek forgiveness for their errors.

But something of far more importance than seeking forgiveness is how a Blademaster responds to making a mistake.

In order to keep on the correct path of service and balance, a Blademaster needs to be able to learn from their error so that, in the future, they will be able to make the correct choice when presented with a similar situation.

A Blademaster should also be able to find a way to correct her mistakes when she makes them. This is, perhaps, the hardest part of this law. But it is important that the Blademaster who makes a mistake find a way to make things right again.

That is the only way to stay on the path of the Light.

The Twentieth Law
of the Blades

A Blademaster is measured by the companions that she keeps. Choose your inner circle carefully.

Despite all of the abilities a Blademaster has, she cannot, by the very nature of the conflicts she will have to endure, do everything on her own. She will need to depend on others in order to do all that she will be required to do.

The Blademaster should find the right people to surround herself with. The right companions will help her immensely. The wrong companions will hinder her ability to do as she must.

She must exercise excellent discernment in the people that she comes in contact with. Some people are meant to be in her life, while others are not. A Blademaster must be careful in determining which is which.

the twenty first law of the blades

he Blademasters only owe fealty to the balance. They serve only the Southern Dales. Their only quest is for the truth. Only in this way can they fulfill their purpose.

Truth and balance are the only true masters a Blademaster has. A Blademaster must always seek and speak the truth. Truth and wisdom are guides to a Blademaster's purpose, and they will guide her in such a fashion as to be able to truly serve the Southern Dales.

Always verify the veracity of things. Always seek to learn new things. And always seek out new ways to serve the Southern Dales.

A Blademaster must always seek to be in balance in herself so that she can find balance in her service. She must always speak truth in her own life so that when she speaks to others in the course of her service, she always speaks the truth to them.

By being in balance and committing to the truth, a Blademaster guarantees that she will always be fit to serve the people of the Southern Dales.

The Twenty Second Law of the Blades

Sometimes the right decisions are the hardest ones to make.

As they go through their duties to the Southern Dales, the Blademasters will be required to make many choices. Many of these choices will be hard to make.

The hardest, and in many ways the most important, will be the ones that affect the lives of others. Many of the decisions a Blademaster will be called on to make will be life or death decisions for others. It is important that these decisions be taken with care. Regardless of how a Blademaster prepares to make such a decision, they will be the hardest ones for her to make.

Can a Blademaster, for instance, go to a city to save people if she knows that, by doing so, she condemns the entire region to war? Who would it be better to save in that instance? (I find it ironic that you wrote this considering you condemned me for going to Willowdale to save the people of Valendale, which was absolutely the right decision. –Alana)

The best way for a Blademaster to make such a decision is to let wisdom and the Laws of the Blades guide her in her decision. The Law of the Blades and the wisdom of Taelin will always guide a Blademaster to the correct choice, no matter how difficult a decision it will be.

The Twenty Third law
of the blades

he war never ends. Only the battles change.

So long as there are representatives of the Light and of the Dark, there will be conflict between the two. The war between the Light and the Dark is a constant, ever changing battle. The Blademasters will, by their nature of being the chosen warriors of the Light, be in the center of that ever changing battle.

As long as the Blademasters exist, they will fight that battle, but the battle will take different forms. At times, the battle can be a direct battle with the forces of the Dark God. At other times, it could be a political battle to keep the Southern Dales on the path of the Light.

The Laws of the Blades

No matter what form the battle takes, the Blademasters will have to fight it constantly as they go through their day to day activities.

It is, unfortunately, a fact of life that this battle is never ceasing, but that is why the Blademasters are so important to the Southern Dales.

the twenty fourth law of the blades

ll actions have consequences.

Every action that is made by anyone in the world has consequences, whether those consequences are for the person whose actions they were or for someone else. These consequences can be good or bad, but there is no way to avoid consequences.

For the Blademasters, though, those consequences can be much larger as their actions can affect many people. It is important to know that a Blademaster's actions can have consequences for many people. There could be instances where a Blademaster's actions can have consequences for the entire Southern Dales.

A Blademaster must not fear the consequences of her actions. Fear of consequences could lead to inaction. And sometimes doing the right thing could have dire consequences. There is no way around this. The Blademaster and her Protector must be ready to face the consequences of their actions.

Some may think it would be better to know what the consequences of actions would be prior to making those decisions. Some think that it is better to meet the consequences head on without knowing what is coming. Either way, the consequences must be faced.

Part of being a Blademaster is living up to the responsibility of facing difficult decisions and living with the consequences of those choices. It is not an easy thing to bear, but the Blademasters must be able to do so.

The Twenty Fifth Law of the Blades

ll things must end.   Nothing remains forever.

At first blush, the Twenty Fifth Law of the Blades seems to directly contradict the Twenty Third Law of the Blades. After all, how can there be one Law that says, "the war never ends" when this Law reads "all things must end" and both be correct?

It is true that there is a mild contradiction between the two Laws, but both are true. For as long as there are two sides to the life on Calthea, there will be the war between good and evil. Thus, the Twenty Third Law of the Blades is, in fact, correct.

The Laws of the Blades

The gods tell us that everything will end one day. They say that even they, themselves, will one day disappear from Calthea. In that, this Law is also correct.

What does this Law mean for the Blademasters, though?

In the case of the Blademasters, it means that all situations that they enter have a resolution. There are no problems that the Blademasters can encounter that are permanent in nature. It is important for the Blademasters to understand that. By knowing that a problem is not permanent means that there is a solution for them to find. This knowledge will allow the Blademaster to use their sharpened mind to figure out that solution.

The Twenty sixth law of the blades

Never hesitate once a course of action has been decided upon. Follow through on all decisions, no matter what the consequences might be.

As she goes through her day to day actions in her service to the balance, a Blademaster will be forced to make many decisions. Some will be large, and others will be small.

All of these decisions will be important to her mission, and all of these decisions must be followed through on.

Decisions have consequences and a Blademaster must follow through on her decisions she makes no matter what the consequences of that decision will be. The Blademaster should not fear the consequences of her decision but

The Laws of the Blades

should follow through with her decisions and face the consequences head on.

the twenty seventh law of the blades

ven though a Blademaster can be put into a leadership role, she must remember that she is meant to serve the balance and the Southern Dales.

I have discussed in these pages many a time that the life of a Blademaster is one of service. She must serve the Southern Dales and she must serve the balance.

There may be times when a Blademaster is put in a position of leadership for the sake of the Southern Dales. While this may be the case, she should only take on such a leadership role if it will help her in her role of service. A Blademaster should not actively seek out a leadership role in the Southern Dales.

The Laws of the Blades

A Blademaster should aspire to leading the Southern Dales through service, not through being in a position of authority over the citizens of the Southern Dales.

the twenty eighth law of the blades

nowledge of the past is the key to the future. Learning from what has come before can lead a Blademaster to the right path and keep her from repeating mistakes made by those who have come before.

Knowledge of prior events is of paramount importance to a Blademaster as she goes forth in her journeys. There are many instances wherein things that have happened before will happen again.

Knowledge, though, is power. It is important that a Blademaster learn the way things happened before so that she is armed with the knowledge she needs to make the correct decisions in any given situation.

The Legacy of the Blademasters will be a living library that the Blademasters will be able to consult in order to be able to have the knowledge they need to make the right choices.

It is important that the Blademasters fully understand the purpose of the Legacy of the Blademasters and embrace the importance of being a part of it.

the twenty ninth law of the blades

ictory must be deserved to be earned. A Blademaster must always fight her battles with honor and love. Even so, victory is never guaranteed. But only by fighting with honor and love can a Blademaster hope for victory in her battles, whether they be physical, mental, or emotional.

By the nature of her life, a Blademaster must constantly deal with conflict, whether it be conflict of the mind, body or emotions. A Blademaster must be prepared to fight all of those battles as they come up.

In order for the Blademasters to have any hope of victory in their day to day battles, they must approach each battle the same. Only by fighting with honor, can they hope to be victorious.

But a Blademaster must be prepared to fail even by fighting with honor and love. Conflict, by its very nature, is violent and unpredictable. Honor gives the Blademaster the best possible chance to conquer that violent unpredictability.

the thirtieth law of the blades

n her service to the Southern Dales, a Blademaster can be called upon to sacrifice anything she has, up to and including her life, if it means preserving the balance. Such sacrifice will never be demanded out of malice. Such a sacrifice, should it be called for, must be made willingly and out of a spirit of love.

A life of service is a life of sacrifice, whether it be a sacrifice of physical possessions, a sacrifice of how one would have their life go otherwise, or even sacrifice of one's life.

Sacrifice comes from love. It is because of that that Blademasters may be called on to make personal sacrifices as they go through their journeys. There is no joy in requiring sacrifices from the Blademasters. But if a Blademaster lives in the First Law of the Blades, such sacrifices will be made willingly.

A Blademaster may be called on to give her life for others. As with any other sacrifice, sacrifice of self, should it be called for, should be made willingly and out of love instead of obligation.

The Final Law
of the Blades

n all that they do, the Blademasters and their Protectors are in service to the world. It is their obligation to leave Calthea in a better condition than it was upon their birth.

All of the previous Laws lead into this one Final Law of the Blades. If the Blademasters live their lives according to the precepts set down in the remainder of the Laws of the Blades, then they will, by the very nature of living their lives in the Law of the Blades, fulfill this final Law.

It is the mission of the Blademasters to improve the condition of the world through their service. It could take as little as touching one life to accomplish this, but the Blademasters should strive to leave the world a better place because they were a part of it.

The Laws of the Blades

Love all you come in contact with, whether they be friend or foe. Be kind to all you come in contact with. Forgive when necessary. Ask for your own forgiveness when you have wronged others. Do all these things, and you will succeed in leaving the world a better place.

final thoughts

hus concludes the Law of the Blades. The Law of the Blades is inviolate for the Blademasters. It is my hope that the Law of the Blades will truly help the Blademasters in their task of service to the Southern Dales.

I cannot stress the importance that the Law of the Blades has in the life of a Blademaster. And yet, it is imperative that the Blademasters discover the truth of the Law of the Blades on their own. Were they to just read these words, the Law of the Blades would not have the same import to them as learning the Law of the blades as they go.

Therefore, this document shall remained sealed in the sanctuary of the High Priestess of the Blades. The day may come when the full text of the Law of the Blades is given to the Blademasters. But that day is far afield in the future.

I have written this document in the hopes that my thoughts will one day help a Blademaster.

The Laws of the Blades

Written by my own hand,

Solara Moonfire

High Priestess of the Blades

The Law of the Blades is not a rigid set of laws to hold the Blademasters to. Lady Solara has meant well, but she never truly understood the purpose of the Law of the Blades.

The Law of the Blades is meant as a guide to aid the Blademasters as they go through life. It is meant as a code to live up to, not as a rigid and binding set of laws. The Blademasters would do well to read Lady Solara's thoughts on the Law of the Blades, but it is up to each individual Blademaster to truly understand how best to apply the Law of the Blades to their life.

Having lived in the Law of the Blades, I can assure the Blademasters reading this that their lives WILL be better for applying the concepts of the Law of the Blades to their lives and their journeys. They will find that living in love, as the First Law of the Blades says to, will make everything easier.

And so, I am ensuring that future Blademasters read these words, both Lady Solara's and mine, in the hopes that their lives will be enriched by the Law of the Blades.

Written by my own hand,

Alana Steeldrake

Master Blademaster
Written during the War of Souls

The books

The Legacy of the Blademasters

The Legend of Raven Windrider
1 Part 1: The First Blademaster

The Blademaster Chronicles

1 The Blademaster
2 Willowdale
3 The Age of Darkness
4 Dragonsbane
5 The Revenge of the Zeraphim

Legends of Calthea

The Laws of the Blades
Heartstone

The Laws of the Blades

About the Author

Rick Bentsen released his first novel in 2001. It was a simple science fiction story that was somewhat well received. Although it never sold very well, the people that read his first novel enjoyed it immensely. From that first moment, Rick was hooked.

Rick has long loved science fiction and fantasy books and movies and that love has turned into a writing passion. He has recently added a mystery/thriller series to his normal science fiction and fantasy series as projects to complete.

Rick lives in southeastern Massachusetts which he believes is the most beautiful place in the world. Fall in New England, he finds to be the most inspirational time of the year with all the colors.

Rick can be reached through his facebook page (www.facebook.com/RickBentsenAuthor) or through his webpage (www.rickbentsen.com) You can buy autographed copies of his books at www.mkt.com/RickBentsen and join his Patreon page at www.patreon.com/RickBentsen

www.ingramcontent.com/pod-product-compliance
Lightning Source LLC
Chambersburg PA
CBHW032025040426
42448CB00006B/723